W9-AKD-611

HAYDN

For Ali, Jojo and Ben

First edition for the United States, Canada,
and the Philippines published 1992
by Barron's Educational Series, Inc.

Design David West Children's Book Design

© Copyright by Aladdin Books Ltd 1992
Copyright in the text © Ann Rachlin / Fun with Music

Designed and produced by
Aladdin Books Ltd
28 Percy Street
London W1P 9FF

All rights reserved
No part of this book may be reproduced in any form
by photostat, microfilm, xerography, or any other
means, or incorporated into any information retrieval
system, electronic or mechanical, without the written
permission of the copyright owner.

All inquiries should be addressed to:
Barron's Educational Series, Inc.
250 Wireless Boulevard
Hauppauge, NY 11788

International Standard Book No. 0-8120-4988-8

Library of Congress Catalog Card No.92-9521

Library of Congress Cataloging-in-Publication Data
Rachlin, Ann.
Haydn / by Ann Rachlin : illustrations by Susan Hellard. --1st
ed. for the U.S., Canada, and the Philippines.
p. cm. -- (Famous children series)
Summary: Focuses on the childhood and early musical training of
the eighteenth-century Austrian composer, Joseph Haydn.
ISBN 0-8120-4988-8
1. Haydn, Jospeh. 1732-1809--Childhood and youth--Juvenile
literature. 2. Composers--Austria--Biography--Juvenile literature.
[1. Haydn, Jospeh. 1732-1809--Childhood and youth. 2. Composers.]
I. Hellard, Susan. ill. II. Title. III.Series: Rachlin, Ann
Famous children series.
ML3930.H3R3 1992
780'.92--dc20   92-9521
[B]   CIP AC MN

Printed in Belgium
67890 9876543

Famous Children

HAYDN

Ann Rachlin
ILLUSTRATED BY Susan Hellard

BARRON'S

3 1489 0041 7 3337

Little Joseph Haydn loved music. In the evening after work his father, Matthias, liked to play the harp. Joseph would sit on his tiny wooden stool with two pieces of wood in his hands. They were his pretend violin. He longed to play a real one.

One day, in 1738, a visitor came to Joseph's house. It was Matthias's cousin, Franck. He was

a schoolteacher who also arranged the music for his local church. Joseph loved listening to him play the violin. After supper Father Haydn and Cousin Franck played together. And Joseph pretended to play with them on his pieces of wood.

When Joseph went to bed, Cousin Franck said, "Joseph is a bright boy. He keeps perfect time and has a lovely voice. He should have music lessons. Let him come and live with me and I will teach him how to play the violin and how to sing." Joseph's mother and father were sad to let their little boy leave home. But they packed his bags and waved as six-year-old Joseph left happily for Cousin Franck's house in Hainburg.

It was hard work. Joseph had to study books, learn to sing with the other boys in Cousin Franck's school, and practice the violin and the clavier, a keyboard instrument something like a piano.

At home, Joseph's mother made sure he was always clean and neat. But here, nobody looked after his clothes. Sometimes they got dirty, however hard he tried to keep them clean. Joseph hated that. He didn't get enough to eat either and he was often hungry. But he soon forgot his hunger when he was singing with the others in church, wearing his special choirboy's wig.

One day an important visitor arrived at the school. He was looking for a boy to sing in his cathedral choir and had heard about talented young Joseph. The visitor's name was Mr. Reutter. All the boys sang for him. Soon it was Joseph's turn.

On the table was a bowl of cherries. Joseph kept looking at them as he sang. At the end Mr. Reutter said,

"You have a lovely voice – I will choose you! As soon as you are eight, you must come and sing in the choir at St. Stephen's Cathedral in Vienna!" and he popped some cherries into the hungry little boy's mouth.

Joseph had never seen anything as magnificent as St. Stephen's Cathedral. But now he had to work even harder. His voice was so good that soon he was singing all the solos. Sometimes, when the service was over and the choirboys were going back to school, Mr. Hermann the baker would call to them.

"You sang very well today, Joseph! Come inside and taste my fresh raisin buns." What a treat!

By this time Joseph was composing music in his head. He wanted to write it down, but he didn't know how. While the other boys were playing games together, Joseph would study alone.

One day an invitation to the palace came from the Empress Maria Theresa. She wanted to hear the boys sing. After singing, the boys went for a walk in the palace garden. Builders had left some ladders there.

"Race you to the roof!" cried Joseph. And they all began to climb.

"Come down at once!" called an angry voice. It was the Empress. "Never do that again! It is far too dangerous!" The boys hurried down.

The next week, when the boys returned to the palace, Joseph looked at the ladders again. He loved climbing.

"Race you to the top!" he cried and up he went. No one else climbed with him.

"How dare you!" It was Mr. Reutter.

"Disobedient boys must be punished!"

Joseph was still trying to write music. Mr. Reutter would not help him.

"Haven't I enough to do," he thundered, "writing music for the Royal Family?"

In desperation, Joseph wrote to his father and mother. They did without food for a week to save enough money for two music books. Night after night, Joseph would read as the others slept.

Joseph was unhappy. His voice had changed. His little brother Michael was singing the solos now. Joseph was bored. He saw a pair of scissors! He picked them up and – snip! He cut off the pigtail of the boy in front of him! Mr. Reutter was so angry that he sent Joseph away from St. Stephen's.

Joseph stood outside the gates of the school. It was cold and dark and he had nowhere to go.

"Hello, Joseph Haydn! What are you doing here at this time of night?" It was his friend Mr. Spangler, who used to sing at St. Stephen's.

Joseph told his friend what had happened.

"You can come and stay in my house if you like," offered Mr. Spangler. "But I can't afford to feed you. You will have to play your violin to earn some money for your food!"

Everyone loved Joseph's music. Then, one day, a letter arrived from a Prince inviting him to live in his palace at Esterhazy and conduct his orchestra.

In the summer the Prince stayed at his country palace. The musicians longed to go back to their families in the city.

"How can we ask the Prince to let us go home?" they asked Joseph Haydn. Joseph started to write some special music.

That night, as the Prince was listening to Joseph's new music, one of the musicians got up, bowed to the Prince and walked away.

"Very strange!" thought the Prince. Then another musician got up and left. And then another.

"Oh! I get the message!" said the Prince. "What a lovely way to ask for a vacation." And he ordered the coaches to take the musicians home immediately.

The musicians loved Joseph and called him "Papa Haydn." At one of his concerts in London, Joseph noticed some people falling asleep because it was late at night. Joseph was not very pleased so he wrote a quiet, pretty tune that made the audience sleepy. But, in the middle, he put in a loud crash that woke them up with a start! Everyone laughed at the joke and stayed awake to enjoy his music. It was "Papa Haydn's Surprise!"

Joseph Haydn wrote 104 symphonies. Many of them had names. Here are some of them.

THE BEAR

THE DRUMROLL

THE LETTER

THE HEN

THE FAREWELL

THE CLOCK

THE SURPRISE

FREEPORT MEMORIAL LIBRARY

3 1489 004 ┃┃┃┃087

J   Rachlin, Ann.
B
Haydn   Haydn.
R

DISCARDED BY
FREEPORT
MEMORIAL LIBRARY

DATE			

FREEPORT MEMORIAL LIBRARY
CHILDREN'S ROOM

BAKER & TAYLOR